An American Voyage

Other books by the author

Guards of the Heart: Four Plays
How To Write or, I used to be in love with my jailer

An American Voyage

Joe Ross

LOS ANGELES
SUN & MOON PRESS
1993

Sun & Moon Press
A Program of The Contemporary Arts Educational Project, Inc.
a nonprofit corporation
6026 Wilshire Boulevard, Los Angeles, California 90036

This book first published in paperback in 1993 by Sun & Moon Press
10 9 8 7 6 5 4 3 2 1
FIRST EDITION
© Joe Ross, 1993
All rights reserved

This book was made possible, in part, through an operational grant
from the Andrew W. Mellon Foundation and through contributions to
The Contemporary Arts Educational Project, Inc.,
a nonprofit corporation

Cover: Thomas Cole, *The Voyage of Life: Manhood*
Reprinted by permission The National Gallery of Art

Some selections of this work have previously appeared in
the magazines *Cathay* and *Texture*. The author wishes to thank
the editors of these publications

LIBRARY OF CONGRESS CATALOGING IN PUBLICATION DATA
Ross, Joe (1960–)
An American Voyage
p. cm — (New American Poetry Series: 12)
ISBN: 1-55713-070-1
I. Title. II. Series.
PS3568.O843487A8 1993
811'.54—dc20
93-34597cip

Printed in the United States of America on acid-free paper.

Without limiting the rights under copyright reserved here, no part of this
publication may be reproduced, stored in or introduced into a retrieval system, or
transmitted, in any form or by any means (electronic, mechanical,photocopying,
recording or otherwise), without the prior written permission of both
the copyright owner and the above publisher of the book.

for my parents

Homage to Past Beginnings

If you took this.
A sensation between want –
And shore.
A deep.
Blue wanting sky.
Waiting water.
Sun
Slowed in revolve of straw.
You taste not the salt or bend
but ride wraps in tight focus of hide.
A change –
perhaps a storm.
Slowing again abating again.
Off shore mountains.
Not speaking here.
Never allowing crest, you cast
a spell, rocks in the casket
an infant's reply.
Long searing sounds of snap –
a tortoise that would not hurt us.
You fell the shell.
A tree you saw.
Not knowing –
No, never knowing.

A king could not be quieted.
You resolved the coral.
A crown ringed with teeth.
Open waters.
Somewhere north is not measured.
This angle has a life of its own.
Just a prism
to hold would be wrong doers.
Not to follow or test.
You're guided by refraction.
An instant before sight standing behind bars.
A green coral grief –
cast upon barren shores.
Just a feeling you said.
Smoke.
Bluesmoke burned.
A cabin or hut.
Thatched ice hacked away –
Here is no language, you said.

Awash or dry –
An island empty of rumor.
A solitary dance.
Rooms lighted by reflection.
Becoming again memory, effaced
thatched in patchwork reply.
Sealed in hot oil.
Igniting one to row.
Or not.
A roof suspended by sequel.
Green fish.
A nearly impossible straw.

A single spark.

Off blue.

                The color is air
                left to resolve its own.
                A long charcoal sweep
                inverting light.
                A glide above the ground.

                                      This vision.
                                      Your vision.

Quiet enough to think.

The waters sent back.
An eggshell
unformed in forgotten wish.

Reeds upon layering reeds
a slight curve in a naked body.
Held so tight the sky vanishes.
Heavy air,
ambiguous breath.

In your will to change –
Only this.

                    Green tropical cups.
                    Half baked bread.
                    You rise only to float again.
                    Not to soar.
                    Unable to find ground,
                    solid in your only sand.

*

This world green blue in ambivalent sound.
The heat pressing down against.
The will of current.
Strings of palm.
Adagio of fish.
A light step into swim
recovering artifice from extinction.
Even the breath blue.
A tongue held in coconut bite,
the skin peeled back.
Raw fruit.
Rare exclamation.
A single purpose.
A lame excuse
limping for the night.
Stars suspended in inverted light.
Something is not right.
Something refuses to listen –
Speak or tell.

Natives on the point of curare.
A tip of flint.
Poison fires.
Sticks crossed across abandoned skulls.
The eyes poked into ice.
A forgotten call to tree –
It moves us.
Still.

All the island inhabited by rain.

Wet, slow, vines.

Swinging in damp silence –
blackness baked by sliced heat,
the opposite of oppression.
You light your own stand.
It does not count.
It never has.

*

The royal song speaks through bushes.
Reeds becoming thickets.
Caught, scraped by admission –
You confess to the immediacy of blue.

*

Along dives –
Misses in the valve.
Choked metal in green flesh.
The trees ripen.
Exposed to fruit.
How hollow
below.

*

Each swim a shade to night.
A homage to impossible flesh.
A long take in rough weather.
The winds so strong.
An erasure of hold.

Here.
Observations become straw.
Floating in the ooze of night.
Resting between where –
And then.
You fumble with lace
a practice out of touch.
Endlessly overseeing.

                    A gull
                    perched in tactile reply.

Each stroke
hot and cool in smoky dissolve.
A lost thought.
A free giving.
Your water turns murky,
a slight dryness in the throat.
It has been years.
A palm points to forgotten shell.

It is –
in the green of cloudy dissolve
an island lost by maps.

                    White, stern, immobile in hold.

A view above.
What stood, lied.
Clamped wrists.
Twisted hair.
A single insertion on the point of old.
A temple.
No where to be found.
Blue underbrush.
The need for palm.
Your knees folded.
Accepting water's lost reply.
A wave let in.
Sand reached.
A building of shore.

Soon.
Mountains.

A dream of dance.
Among the reeds.
Twisted in turquoise abandon.
The air so light it becomes water.
No sense imposed.
Allowing your own.
Overcome by slope.
A tangent to stars.
Your way not mapped.

                Forgotten North.

An emersion into blue,
an understanding of there
and not.

                Majestic fish.

A throne you could not loan.
This fruit, lean.

                Pulpy cores.

A wound exposed to sun.
The salt so dense you refuse the night.
A hut constructed of raw nerves.
A salve for the flesh.
A balm for the body.
You lay your straw,
Sleep –
rest and cry.

Leaning begins.
A slight sway in iron thought.
The nails painted brittle.
An elegant stretch of hand.
You awake to your own wake.
A memory of miles upon a sandy beach.
The sun so warm upon a naked back.
Each step a print into presence.
A single vision upon an exposed thigh.
The lips red, parted.
Each line, moisture for a searching tongue.
This held in mouth –
savored in wide blue's spread light.
A tension on the tip of taut.
You freeze –
Let go.

*

A single lost walk to the edge of dune.
Each foot.
A step into coconut.
Wild wanderings in the wild of stars.
You make a head-spinning turn and stare
wide open to a density of tropical hope.
Some where a front approaches.

Coral longings caught in green.
A slight glance waiting death's reply.
Here, you can float –
Swim into pale resolve of storm.
Pebbles roundly cradled in upon wave's hold.
You cannot wash this.
Clean in forgotten storms.
Fitfully kicking –
water too deep to suspend.

A reed.

                              A single reed
                              Sounding.

Upon the point of recovery,
shoulders straightened.
A flat spine of an unread book.

                    It is ancient.
                    It is near.

Now taken as parting.
Your warm imagination
from the green of wash.
You linger –
allowing imperfect fish.
A tale.
Songs in coral rhyme.
The sleeves pushed up
the hand cupped.
Accepting.
It flows through.
Water's instant reply to breath.

*

It becomes grave.
Flowers laid, not death.

*

A season, always
a season.

A new world pushing through.
Vapor forms in smoky context.
This flows up.
Pulls brown to surface.
A vacuum filled.
Here you have new eyes –
Illumed by the incandescent heat within.
The weather so unsure.
The point
still turning in hapless conviction.
Birth and death, still a rose blooming.
The river runs towards the sea –
Brown, dirty, old, again.
Maybe a God.
Maybe ash.

   *

What dream lives tonight.
A light landing upon surface.
Airy in the way you accept.
Trees in a vast continuum.
Orchids, bouquets of velvet.
You feel it way below.
A pull.

Searching for a vision of new home.
You imagine white washed colors floating in the dark.
Free horses, wilder strawberries.
Image upon image, colliding.
Impinging space.

*

Crowded with trees, tearing petal's forgotten years –
A yearling roaming wild.
Unbridled in flora swamp.
You stop.
Shake your head of unconnected scene.
This screen, dissolving into foam.

You need to look into looking back.
An ancient symmetry.
Prior to.
Locution.
Circles left incomplete.
Euclid assigned a single seat in a long row.
Stars and clocks left standing in the rear.
You see moss upon rocks, upon lava & crystals.
Hyper & hypo, only sounds in seams of waves.
A memory perhaps.
An opening back to what opened before.

You wish a single history.

*

Pale & green in unturned musty page.
Your concentration slips upon a bare rock.
All footing reduced to slides between time.
It is here that beginning begins.
Brothers to a past, Mother to the future.

In a shell –
between tangle and weave.
A warm breath smoky in lost reply.
You imagine this.
As if becoming became.
A long swim –
waves lapping in.
Tides before time's empty hold.
All there.
A complete.

                          Nearer to shore than sound

Maybe.

To walk upon beach's crystal resolve.
A step towards mountain,
and wide caverns silently in flight.
A free fall of form.
Yet not undone.

   *

For the one lucid hour
in the morning
when I miss you.

This can start.

Cut in guided ragged edges,
A space –
clean of remembered tears.
A near perfect edge
where this began.
In the blue of want.
In the green of need.
Each stroke an act of devotion.
You must learn to worship this angle
without a geometry of space.
To make time.
From the beginning.
Again.

As in a dense flora swamp –
The heat pushing in.
All around.
Too sudden to sound.
The gasp from a quick breath.
There leaning.
Upon what you nearly forgot –
The waters so high.

        A blue of wrap
        embracing a submerged thigh –
        between your dream and sky.

Your will too remote –
beyond the strain of green swinging vine.

So you swim.

                    Head down
                    into a frantic search for ground.

A long lost beach.
An isle of imperfect fruit.

    *

This habitat
or not
between want & shore.

A sensation
slowed in an endless lost resolve

               of *choral.*

A rising of voices.
A majestic mountain pushing through the fog.
Ringed with clouds.
It becomes clear.
Each chord a note towards North
and not.
Yet sung in timeless duration.

   *

This floats up.
Heard all at once.

The object is itself & you.
A complicated image between time.
An emotional construct –
completed between the intellect and mind.
Where horses still roam –
feeding on green coral.
An image always turning.
You cannot keep still.
The point slips.
Its own season.
Nothing left blank, always turning
in the open of surging seas.
You struggle to find your breath
for this song.
The union of what you remember
and what you forget.

                      When you suddenly know

The world you made up
in the heat of frozen longing.

                            There you sing.

Not to yourself, not for others –
But to what's there when you're not.

*

You close your eyes
You rub the sand.

A Still Prayer

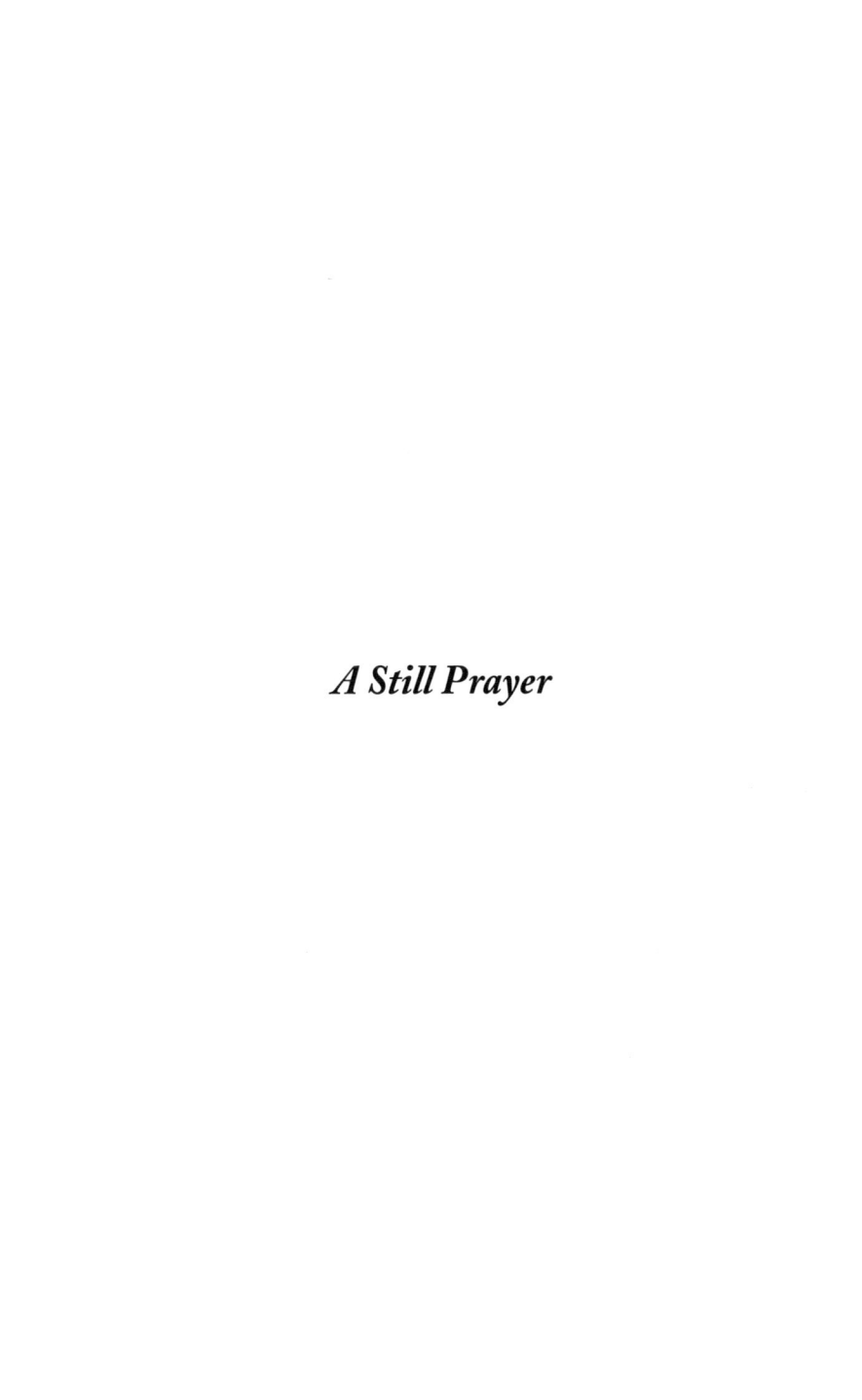

A brown pushing down –

                        Listening to the risings again.

                        Against even the stand of it.
                        When your shell is empty.

You stand looking.
Into several colors of inversion.
A free fall.
Lost in a retreat of white.

   *

Twisted palm, green roots.
You float a diversion into sand.
Nearly closed walls.
An apology to fish.
If you choke here.
An abdication of wreath.
A full mouth.
Months after the fact.
Green and white spaces
lined in full exposure of crystal.
Each faction a fraction of view.
All in – entirely too shallow.
You swallow a need.

Deep in compromise.
You promise an execution of stone.
Bleeding bush.
A hot dry climate of hate.
The finger itching.
Palm sweating.
Too sweet to taste
this dissolution of salt.

Green turning into a black light.
Whole visions sought by rock.
You take any shore as potential.

                                        Home to the longing,
                                        lodging in the throat.

It misses here.
An entire chord caked with mud.
A song about to imagine.

　　*

Connections brought to surface with fire.
Hope crossed with weed.
Blue and black meshing with white.
A new pallet stretched between brushes.
The soundings still.
Echoes born of resonating image.
A hard shell.
An overturned prism.
Here you spoke.
Words about to listen.

　　　　　　　　　　　　If I shook you long enough.

　　　　　　　　　　　　If what was tied became undone.

A single white light.

                                                    Far below from above.

How hopeful, how impenetrably sad.

    *

You, you've cried.

A ship at full sail.
Amassing not between the dockings.
Leaving the shore – leaving the vine.

Slow swinging in the ooze of night.
A firm grip upon a grasp about to.
Out of the stubble of some forgotten stance.

                          When the wind blows.
                          When pebbles turn to rocks.

You rise from a space between.
Mountain and sky meshing with sand.
A new glass half empty of wine.
A single pressure held in hand.
A revolver cocked in full sight.
It turns.
Each snap a sparkle off-white.
Pure cork.
Inverted lead.
A vision seen through lashes.
Striated sight.
Green and brown on its back.
A flipping tongue.
Reason coiled in unspoken throne.
A perfect law of fish.
A current against fin.

A black distance between.
A push at what pushes back.

                                        A cool scene.
                                        From the space of white.

Long drawn figures striding.

You light here.
A flame about to see.

And yet removed.

                        Waves reaching only damp roots.
                        The shore shielded from its sound.
                        This breaks here.

A pure curl into itself –
Foaming white about the mouth.
A hot tongue.
An enlarged seed embedded in sand.
Sinking below the covers.
Sheets pressed in iron hold.
It folds back.
What had become undone.
The head covered.
Feet exposed to the missing below.
Pushing back.
Heat rising from a cool space.
A weightless touch.
An empty hand.

A dance above green broken glass.
Hot coals sliding into sea.
Ashes turning into blue coral.
A vision crowned with escaping breath.
Fleeing mountains.
Melting tundra.
An entire herd migrating towards milk.
This sustains.
From a place of particular patterns.
You come round.
A complete lap.
Circuity felt at synapse's snap.
A sudden flash.
Illuminating a pass.
Re-lived dream not remembered.
How far around a full breaking sound.
In wide open gallop.
Feet embedded in sinking sand.
Each knee bent.
An invitation to color.
You fold your pallet.
Mixing swim and walk.
The doors open.
A breeze let in.

Where light turns –

                              An unspoken sentence
                              Still in the mouth.

A pronouncement of Royal loss.
A footprint melting in unformed crystal.
A clean bowl bending in the night.
New Heads of State –
Salted in lost reply.

*

You acknowledge form.
An empty shadow held in a box
waiting dawn to dispel rumors.

                              Silently said.

The image fractured.
A torture of coral.

Your twisted resolve
left to float in un-named sky.

                              Lost –

between above and brown –
Where light turns back to face.

                                          Long drawn shadows
                                          printed into sand.

A leaden image replete with wire.

    *

Malleable to crown.

                                          A sudden glow
                                          from a forgotten spark.

You listen back.

                                          A cave of conviction.
                                          Bending in the middle.

A dark night followed.
A single reed sounding North.

An escape of breath.

Pushing –
into vines.
You crawl wet with desire.
New brown ground.
An impass of stone sliding in the mouth.

*

If you stop here.
If what was shaken had become undone.

Learning to speak.
In the face of a dream.
A storm approaching.
Tenets held as anchor.
You push back, waiting.

*

The isle –
an inlet to eye.
You tread water, stone.
On your back, head down.
An impossible direction to resolve.

                                                      If North were.

Only singular.
A lost gull.
Back to start.
A tern above the sea.
On a hillside, mountains.
A song to carry.

The capacity to fall.

Stripped voices ringing flat.
An un-named hand miming empty gestures.

*

If it were a different season.
If signs gripped what they held.

                                        A broken image –
                                        and another.

Pieces held in jigsaw silence.

You look hard.
A firm vision about to see.
Your back blistered in unturned sun.
The point laced with suspended air.
You cannot breathe here.
You hear only your own gasp.
Somewhere –

                                              Still
                                              So far away.

          A small space.
          Imagine.

You're held tight in cramped twisted sky.
A so small space this sinking blue.

                              It does not fit.
                              This image, your image.

   *

Just an arm's length.
Nearly able to reach.
Your past, passed out.
No air here.
A quickening into slip.
No name said.
The coral becomes its own.

If you could run with this.
An image between scenes.
And held, still moving.
A free floating lost grasp –
in blue sand.
Your hand able to pluck ungrown flowers.
A wreath laid for a season of king.
The waves break in
turning in inverted sight.
Green coral sounding to fish.
Mountains heard in unbridled reply.
A resonating deep line
anchored in escaping air.
A wide space.
A long ringing composition in brown.
You can understand.
Each pattern speckled with lead.
A prism bending.
An angle hot with degrees of island.

You look deep in.

                        Nearer to the dark –
                        The center brown and then.

You cannot break anymore.

    *

The rules changed.
Permanent erasures penciled in.

When all is free.

                      Several classes of zoo
                      engulfing a singular line.

It is about politics, grammar
And you.

    *

When all is mixed in unwashed resolve.
The deposed, elected, stoned.
Ancient and contemporary shaking in sun.
A tundra melting on a milky beach.
Mountains watching the grain –
Turning from brown to sky.
A wave in purple over seas
shining in reflected coral.
A land of impossible voice.
Adrift in lost community.

And still an island.

Large, foreboding and wet.

Encompassing so many
forgets.

                                        You live here.

Stranded, shaken, and cold.

Below the Surface

A gap.
Seven years wide and more.
At a loss of in between and less.
The stars studded in mixed inverted light.
Objects of worship washed in upon deserted shores.
When all is too suddenly –

                                        Calm, brown –
                                        flailing in green.

A long voyage against rock.
The beginning of angle.
Resonating within prism.

*

If you could bring the world
in a wide stare into white.
The arms opened wider than shoulders allow.
When sex is not sex.
This goes out.
Returned in so many others.
Up-turned in misplaced image.

Rubbing against the edge of it.

The stakes raised.
The roots pulled in brown sound.
A mixing together in dense community.
This land named in unknown call.
Breaking upon nearly deserted shores.

                                        When this goes out.
                                        When you begin.

Alone, washed in deserted recall.
You begin to think back.
A way through.
From the first voyage –
to this landing. A rock.
Tossed from sea to pool.
Our roots disturbed
from the clear reflection
scattered by the waves made
of so small pebble.

                                    When home becomes only place.

Streets crowded with ambush feeling.
Not resting here.
A land of mis-placed hope.
In-operable opportunity.
You set your sites on.
You buy in.

   *

Time's erasure of hold –

                if you give in.

A land lost in concrete block,
unable to face.

The sea's swell
drowning unwanted thought.

*

The edges ripen –
You grab for rotten fruit.

> To get your piece.
> To bake your slice.

*

The center falls in –

The edges collapse in green and brown.
A lost community adrift in stale waters.
Tensions tighten by what was taut.
Becoming undone unable to hold afraid
to be always nearer a stop than sail.
Kept going
spurting against itself.
New ways of travel discovered
outstretching horizon breaks
beyond the line of new.
A world passed proved points
refusing rest upon flat
merits.

A general lack of what's broken back
into the sway
of sound
still
so far away.

*

You choke on it.
Grasping for breath
in the blue and green of ambiguity

                         that will not hold,
                         that cannot hold.

Your land.
Your landing that becomes ours.

The need to be
foregrounded upon a wide stare
into the coral of tropical cups.

Disregarded by kings being
held in wet deposition.

Your image.
Galloping into eloping night
where light does not hold.

It was a simple story.

Cut in abandoned reply.
Longing for the together
which had to become cement.

Trapped by that of which was –

                                  The inverted reflection
                                  of a broken crystal.

    A land of paralysis

            miming only
            miming only empty belief.

The leaning into wind which became fall.

                    Your turning color –
                    into a single blind white light.

Scan if you must the solitary cabin
which became the prison.

The prism of bluesmoke burned,
hacked away, thatched, and cast upon barren shores.

                    Floating in the ice you become
                    the single cube of green fish.

Making room –
rooms for the dance of rumor,
becoming effaced of memory – a sequel to thought.

Needing the spark of a single reed —
A simple sounding to see.

To glide off the ground in unformed wish.

This was the land –

                land of your birth in forgotten eggshell hope.

Newly polished,
a lack of where.

        You fought not here
        to become
        only undone
        by lost connection.

Can you understand.

        This afloat.
        A parade of ancient vine.

Look
strain to see
to return to what turned in
to this lost island
afloat upon borrowed swell.

        *

It was not yours.
Taken in assault of wealth.
The tips unmatched with poisoned firepower lead.
A paralysis set in.
The spirit taken with immobile cure.

> A tone not heard to be majestic.
> A tribal yell at brutal sea.

While the seeds gave up in unplanted harvest.

The haze that becomes you
in a cesspool of moon.

    *

When study becomes only line –

you dissolve into the uncertainty
of wash
before colors became collage.

                    Strips of green upon white
                    before the gesso dried,
                    before the angles bent.

How far beyond a new hung moon
piecing it back into blue
or paler
tears of your unframed thought.

    *

The insistent charm of new language

A way to speak breaking through.
Coiled reason drawn undone by new wine.

                        You sip it.

The ancient tundra upon the tongue.
A frozen beach held in mind.

                        Melting and melding in singular view.

To take to wind
before the breathing stops.

A deep inhalation listening to there.

*

                        It confuses you.

Confounding the drive –
music and your sounding to say it.
To be heard all at once from
unbroken center where the chords vibrate
in untuned want.

You sought what may not hold.

                                      The edges open out.
                                                        The tying becomes undone.

The water's infant deaf reply,
the only wash of unstained color.

    *

It becomes a free floating textual content.
The continent dominant
to determine victors from vectors.
The surface wet with transcendentality
the lateral complexity of modification factors.
The fields pushed in.
Water released for projective consumption.
You head toward a setting sun.

South of North.
The topology of what was to be mapped.
Feeling your way through.
A battle fought between wood and ink.
You assign the reproduction to sign.
The interplay of object
and the object of you as the word you.
Your head spins in lost image.
The outside stays out.
Dominant categories engorged
in synthetic resistance.
You lose sight of the music.
A broken dance in detached experience.
When the language came in

You said.

Staring into the white of an opaque moon –

You could not say its name,
gesturing only incomplete motion.
A wave of the tongue.
A flip of the hand
pointing North or West in meaningless direction.
The ears straining to broken music.
Notes upon coral playing with eyes shut.
Only up to your knees.
Stiff-legged,
frozen.

*

Inertia inherited without intent
in the illusion of open possibility.
The story ends in broken bits
tossed from lineage to lien.
The place not owned
assumed at birth.
The right manifested in conquering destiny.
From where you came
in displaced homogeneity
to know nothing of what you are.

When kinetic turns to frantic
from the outside in not released.
Turned again upon yourself.
You cannot hear
that it all matters.
Everyone
in upon without.
You cannot choose between.
From where you came
to trust outside.
Wide open windows balanced
upon sills,
silly views.

                                      The safety of a foreign coast.

When diversity leads to division.
The egg splits in unfertile ground
cast among players in stone.
The weeds grow back between –

                                      One coast
                                      and another.

When it is not deep enough.
When couplets break single into long lines.
Your voice cracks.
Music leaves your ears.

You come to know war
only from the side –
lines drawn straight with discord,
dissonance mixed with ease among vulnerability.

> The spine firm,
> The page unstained.

A people without history
riding the surface of unbroken wave.

> Easy to be confused
> Mis-directed.

When you go hot and cold.
Trees bent in dis-illusioned wave.
A flag reflected in ghost silence shimmer.
Plastic covers what can be seen through.

> The holes are wide
> spanning the arms.

Striated in crested seal.

Your coat is not warm.
The campfire replaced by cathode light.

Nothing touches you –
Feelings played in mock courage.

                                        You were taught to run.

            Dive for cover
            in sterile stride.

*

Your pose, a question.
Lips unmoved.
Mouth agape.
Teeth clenched in fisted wait.

                                  You do not feel the bite.
                                  Incision slowed
                                  to imperceptible pain.

Cutting through –
fibers un-revealing at the core.

*

Where is the language,
you wanted to ask.

To find a voice –

        Speaking along with a nearly forgotten past.
        Singing from the edge of sea
        to new lands
        found through deaf fog.

    *

        A music without malice.
        A siren only to speed the course.

You can hear this –
a port becoming yours.

*

At work so long –
an ethic assumed for lack of peace.

The shoulder to rest the burden
in blame's pointing fault.

                                          You are free
                                          to
                                          flail.

On your back
unblistered and inured –

                                          humanity runs off.

The burden
squarely on you.
A beast created
to waste.

This taken land is what you come to inherit.

                    Divested of history
                    a place
                    placed out of beginning.

Still unreflected
in slant of light.

                    A spin upon account –
                    Myth removed in projected space.

A tube imparts what you cannot chew.

*

You swallow it whole.
You curse the consequence.

You must take the risk —

                    Through several layers of fragmentation.

    *

A dance around what might have been dead
To feel again
where words will not hide.

                    A run on history.
                    Your history.

Struggling to piece together —
what was before this could be.

                    Where you spoke
                    of the green
                    in a blue coral sea.

To feel again

the pull of a pull
of the wave of a wash
of the wash
over you

                      before you break

    *

upon the break of a nearly broken
shore you knew
to be the last
of the last of the lost
of the land before the sea

                              You struggled to see

to find the land of the fought
to remove the shards
of your scattered struggle
to breathe a pure past

                                        to paste it together

to begin before the strangle
in a web woven in waters tight
to conceal the fight that was fought
by those wrought imperceptible

by your language's languish
at the surface
of survival

                              you allowed humanity to float
                              upon a float destined to breech

any truth of any shore of any hope
you may have reached

      *

        There you spoke –
        unable to hold your tongue

    Still

You would not allow the gloss
of the loss of all that you were
before.

                You spoke, again
                you raised up your voice,
                and you spoke, again.

And blew into a tearing wind
that truth will not hide
forever hidden
by the gloss
of the surface without a land
that became to be called land.

The landing of all you knew to be true.

                                A flat empty float upon the surface
                                of the skim of what you skimmed.

And called truth
the empty place to root
the exploiting that you followed
without intervention to recall
the call you once knew how to make
before it all breaks.

                                You must not allow this anymore.

    *

You inhale deep.
You rub your eyes.

                  And
                  You speak.

New American Poetry Series (NAP)

1. *Fair Realism,* Barbara Guest
2. *Some Observations of a Stranger at Zuni in the Latter Part of the Century,* Clarence Major
3. *A World,* Dennis Phillips
4. *A Shelf in Woop's Clothing,* Mac Wellman
5. *Sound As Thought,* Clark Coolidge
6. *By Ear,* Gloria Frym
7. *Necromance,* Rae Armantrout
8. *Loop,* John Taggart
9. *Our Nuclear Heritage,* James Sherry
10. *Arena,* Dennis Phillips
11. *I Don't Have Any Paper So Shut Up,* Bruce Andrews
12. *An American Voyage,* Joe Ross
13. *Into Distances,* Aaron Shurin
14. *Sunday's Ending Too Soon,* Charley George

For a complete list of our poetry publications
write us at Sun & Moon Press
6026 Wilshire Boulevard
Los Angeles, California 90036